The Go
Collectors Handbook

Editor
Francis Joseph

Contributors
Lynne Godding
Eve & John Rossiter
Kath Burns

Francis Joseph Publications
ISBN 1-870703-89-8

Acknowledgements

A special thank you to Lynne Godding whose enthusiasm as a Golly Collector made this book possible. Also thanks to Eve and John Rossiter who allowed me to photograph their collection and Kath Burns who produced much of the detail and most of the prices to the pictured items.

It has been a fascinating project to research the beginnings of the Golly. As he is no longer a participant in the commercial world, he still remains as a fond but distant memory, and will be much sought after for his obvious innocent appeal in the years to come.

As this is the first time we have attempted this guide, there will inevitably be errors and omissions for which I take full responsibility. I apologise unreservedly for these and welcome any help and advice that you collectors may like to give in order that the second edition is a more complete publication.

Francis Joseph

The Golly Collectors Handbook
© 2003 Francis Joseph Publications
1st edition

Published in the UK by
Francis Joseph Publications
5 Southbrook Mews, London SE12 8LG
Telephone: 020 8318 9580

Typeset by E J Folkard Computer Services
199 Station Road, Crayford, Kent DA1 3QF

Printed by
Red Design and Print Ltd, England

ISBN 1-870703-89-8

Contents

Introduction

This Golly Collectors Handbook gives an insight into the world of the Golly after over 100 years as a children's companion. He is still loved and appreciated by a great number of people around the world. The photographs taken from personal collections here, show a selection of items that have been available over the years.

Florence Upton was born in 1873 to English parents in New York. It was when Florence introduced a 'Golliwogg' into one of her illustrated books, in 1895, that the Golly first came into children's literature. In her first book, Florence wrote about two wooden Dutch dolls, and introduced a character called 'Golliwogg'. This character was described as a gnome, and actually looks quite scary with his mass of black hair, huge head, button eyes and pointed nose. As if to reinforce his toyland status, he is always illustrated like a teddy bear with paws instead of hands – he has no fingers or thumb. There is something about his character and his mischievous nature that makes him a real star from the outset. This first book is simply entitled: 'Two Dutch Dolls', and it is now very rare and very collectable, as are all the others. The name 'Golliwogg' is not even mentioned in the title of the first book, but so strong and likeable was the character that he was introduced in subsequent illustrated books by Florence Upton, and his name appears in the title on all future publications. Her illustrated series of books, with verses written by her mother, Bertha, became huge sellers – and the 'Golliwogg' became a popular childhood toy, symbolic of the innocence and mischief of a child. Looking through the original quarto books, one cannot help but be captivated by this charming toytown character. The designs are lovely and charming, and full of life. It was to be the beginning of an era that has all but passed us by. By the 1930s the golly even became a symbol of love and would appear on Valentine cards that men would send to their sweethearts. Some of these are shown in this book.

In Britain, the popularity of the Golly was furthered by John Robertson, the son of James Robertson the preserve manufacturer. He had noticed just how popular golly dolls were with children during his visit to North America. He brought one back, and it became a firm favourite with his own children. He thought it would make an ideal mascot, and it was consequently agreed that the Golly would become the company's trademark. One of the earliest badges to be produced was made from Bakelite with a pin fixed to its back. Unfortunately not many of these have survived, as they were easily broken. In 1924 tin badges, painted with a white waistcoat, red trousers, and blue jacket replaced them. Some wore a leather hat and others had hair glued to their heads. It wasn't until 1928 that the first enamel brooch 'The Jolly Golly Golfer' was produced. This was to be the start of a very popular and successful collecting scheme, with millions of badges being produced over the years. Of course many collectors of gollies simply collect these badges, and the multitude of variations that are possible between one badge and the next makes identification very difficult. Colin Dodds checklists on this subject are best to pour over in this case. We urge you to contact him at the following address for more detailed information on the Robertsons badges than we are able to provide in this book: Colin Dodds, 10 Woodcroft, Kennington, Oxford, OX1 5NH

Apart from rag dolls, badges and illustrations, there are lovely dolls from Merrythought and Steiff, figurines of gollies from Carlton Ware and Silver Crane, teasets, ephemera of all kinds, even lovely perfume bottles.

During the 1970s and 80s, Golly became a controversial figure as the name of this loveable toy was hijacked by racist people. To many he remained simply a bright cheerful toy, but was labelled by some as the cause of the offence and he was consequently withdrawn from general circulation. Some publishers went as far as re writing children's books, replacing him with an alternative character – even Enid Blyton, the popular childrens writer, was censored. Consequently the golly, misrepresented and misunderstood, has been removed from popular culture. Such was his popularity though, that Robertson's retained Golly as their mascot until the new millennium. Now they have updated their promotions to include characters from Roal Dahl.

However, the announcement of Golly's withdrawal has coincided with a more relaxed attitude to this simple, ineffectual toy. Recently there has been evidence of a revival with Golly collectibles appearing in gift shops, and the occasional sighting of Golly Dolls appearing alongside Teddies in toyshops. Also, the new Carlton Ware golly series is proving very popular with collectors, and there are plans for a new series of gollies based on Florence Upton's original designs. Robertson's dropping of their mascot has in fact refuelled interest in him, further making him highly sought after in the world of collectables. So if you think you may have a few golly items in your loft, now is the time to search them out.

Recently, prices of gollies across the board have gone up dramatically. Particularly in the case of badges. Ebay, the internet auction site, is a great place 'bid' on certain items. But please beware, auction prices vary enormously and so the prices reached cannot be taken seriously – they simply reflect the price that a particular buyer is willing to pay. Pre-war badges seem to sell for the most amount of money, ranging from anywhere between £100 and £500 per item, with limited edition sets following closely behind. We have put some prices of badges in this book, but please beware that although these prices have genuinely been reached at auction, they are specific to that item, sold at that time.

We must also add that in some cases there are fake Robertsons badges on the market. Please beware that although Robertsons have dropped the Golly from their brand image, they still hold the copyright to their original designs and will take steps to protect their image. Fake Robertsons badges are like fake money – they are counterfeit and it is not only illegal to make them, but also to sell them on.

It is true to say that all Golly memorabilia has considerably increased in value but it is still possible to find a bargain. However, If you are thinking about becoming a collector, you would be strongly advised to join a Golly Collectors Club and to visit one of the many Golly Web sites available. These are regularly updated and if you are unsure of the value or the availability of an item, they contain all the information you need.

When adding to your collection. It is worth remembering that you should not think about how much the item may be worth in the future, but of how much it means to you now. Therefore if its value should increase, it will be a bonus. If, on the other hand, it doesn't you will not be disappointed.

Francis Joseph

Golly Ephemera

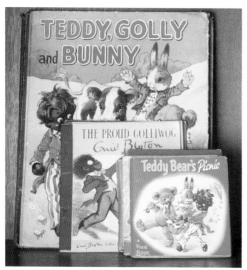

Three 1950s books featuring golly, illustrated by Kennedy and Enid Blyton. These books are fairly plentiful and easy to find but only books in very good condition are of interest to collectors. Teddy, Golly and Bunny, A E Kennedy £45-£55/$65-$85. The Proud Golliwogg, Enid Blyton £10-£15/$15-$23; Teddy Bears Picnic £10-£12/$15-$18.

Collectors set issued in 1995 comprising Eric Horne's wooden peg doll and a fully jointed golly. £150/$220.

Vigny boxed perfume bottle £200-£225/$295-$345. Florence K Upton book published in 1890 by Longman and Greene, and introducing Golliwogg for the very first time, The Adventures of Two Dutch Dolls £275-£350/$405-$535; 1960s reprints in small format The Adventures of Two Dutch Dolls, £55-£75/$80-$115; Florence K Upton Golly Card game, early 1900s, £150-£175/$220-$270.

One of a series of twelve golly books illustrated by Florence Upton, this is the very first book featuring golly and it was printed in 1895. £275-£350/$405-$535.

One of a series of twelve golly books illustrated by Florence Upton and reprinted in the 1960s. The Golliwoggs Polar Adventures £55-£75/$80-$115.

Florence K Upton Golliwogg Advertisement for the publications of the Golliwogg's Bicycle Club 1896, rare item £125-£150/$185-$230.

Raphael Tuck postcard taken from the original drawings by Florence Upton, one of a series copied from her original Golliwogg book, The Adventures of Two Dutch Dolls *and posted 1904. £45/$65.*

Raphael Tuck postcard taken from the original drawings by Florence Upton, one of a series copied from her original Golliwogg book, "The Golliwoggs auto-go-cart" and posted 1903. £45/$65+.

"The Naughty Golly" squeaky book from around the 1920s. The illustrations are thought to be by Agnes Richardson. £45/$65.

A selection of beautiful 1920s Golly Valentines cards made in Germany, £35-£50/$50-$75.
.

Early 1900s Christmas greetings card illustrated by artist, Agnes Richardson, £20-£30/$30-$45.

1929 Agnes Richardson postcard featuring girl and her golly and wording; "I'se got someone to love, anyway", £12/$20+.

OFF TO THE BEACH.

"Off to the beach" one of a series of postcards printed by Valentines and illustrated by Mabel Lucy Attwell. Posted in 1923, £45/$65+.

WAS MAN AUS LIEBE TUT .

"Was man aus liebe tut - - ". German postcard printed in the 1920's and illustrated by Mabel Lucy Attwell. £40/$60+.

THE NEW LOVE
"Never morning wore to evening
But some heart did break."

"The new love" postcard printed by Valentines and illustrated by Mabel Lucy Attwell. Posted in 1922. £40/$60+.

I hope you'll have heaps of presents

"I hope you'll have heaps of presents" Celesque series postcard illustrated by artist Agnes Richardson and posted in 1913. £20/$30+.

Valentine's Golly Postcards, £35-£50/$50-$75.

Valentine's Golly Postcards, £35-£50/$50-$75.

Valentine's Golly Postcards, £35-£50/$50-$75.

Early 1900s Christmas greetings card, £20-£30/$30-$45.

Lovely 1930s postcards £30/$45+.

Obviously part of a series £30/$45.

Golly Ephemera

"Oh golly it's just lovely" postcard illustrated by an unknown artist and posted in the 1930s. £30/$45+.

"Just look at our sunflower" Salmon postcard illustrated by Linda Edgerton from the 1920s. £30/$45+.

Comic postcard printed in 1928 by HB Ltd. By an unknown artist "GEF". £35/$50+.

£20/$30+.

1913 postcard by unknown artist printed in Germany and showing young girl brushing her golly's hair with the words; "Be kind one to another". £12/$20+

Raphael Tuck Christmas greetings postcard from 1910 showing girl and golly with mistletoe and the wording; "And I'm so shy". £12/$20+.

From an original Florence Upton illustration. £30/$50+.

Florence Upton Books

llustrated by Florence K Upton, verses written by her mother Bertha Upton.

Prices £275-£350 up to £800-£1000 for the Golliwogg's Christmas which is the hardest edition to find.

1	1895	The Adventures of Two Dutch Dolls
2	1896	The Golliwoggs Bicycle Club
3	1898	The Golliwogg at the Seaside
4	1899	The Golliwogg in War!
5	1900	The Golliwogg's Polar Adventure
6	1901	The Golliwogg's Auto-go-cart
7	1902	The Golliwogg's Air-ship
8	1903	The Golliwogg's Circus
9	1904	The Golliwogg in Holland
10	1905	The Golliwogg's Fox Hunt
11	1906	The Golliwogg's Desert Island
12	1907	The Golliwogg's Christmas
13	1909	The Golliwogg's in the African Jungle

The Vege-men's Revenge was published in 1897, alas this book is not about the Golliwogg.

The Florence Upton designs are truly lovely. The scenes depicted here are from The Adventures of Two Dutch Dolls, The

Golliwogg in Holland, The Golliwogg's Circus, The Golliwogg's Auto go-cart, The Golliwogg in War! *and* The

Golliwogg at the Seaside. *Here we see him in his adventures, getting into all sorts of scrapes and always very much revered*

Florence Upton Gallery

by his compatriots. Some of these pictures are taken from the original books. Often the binding has come loose and each picture

is then mounted for display. These originals would be worth around £20/$35 each, which is still very reasonable. Here you clearly

see the button eyes and the 'paws' for hands and feet. The Golliwoggs adventures are sweet and innocent and slightly mischievous,

and he appears in many guises. The verses by Bertha Upton are equally merry. Although she would not make a prize winning

poet, the rhymes are simple and enchanting. There are often quite interesting illustrations which go with the verses, though these

are not in colour.

Golly upsets the cheese cart.

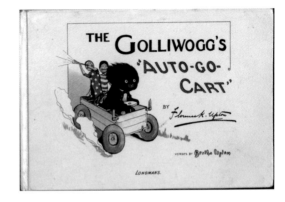

A lovely picture of Golly tiptoeing through the tulips.

Two contrasting images of the Golly. The picture of Golly going to prison is my personal favourite.

Florence Upton Gallery

Who would have guessed that trouble lurked
That morning ride to mar;
Yet,punctured tire has often been
To happiness a bar.

"There! calm yourselves!" says Golliwogg,
"I'll pump it up once more;
This is a very simple thing,
Don't worry, I implore."

Florence Upton Gallery

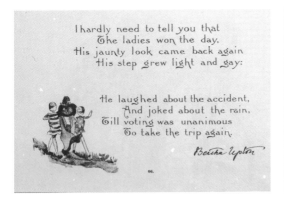

I hardly need to tell you that
The ladies won the day,
His jaunty look came back again
His step grew light and gay:

He laughed about the accident,
And joked about the rain,
Till voting was unanimous
To take the trip again.

Bertha Upton

66.

The ADVENTURES
of two
DUTCH
DOLLS.

BY
FLORENCE
K.
UPTON

Words by Bertha Upton

Golly is introduced for the first time in the picture above. You can see that the two Dutch Dolls are immediately startled. Soon,

Florence Upton Gallery

all that is forgotten, and they begin to party.

In half an hour the sun comes up,
And shows a merry face:
  He winks an eye
  As passing by
He sees the skating place

    And when he peeps into the shop
    With jolly laughing eye,
      Tho' he's not blind
      He cannot find
    A single toy awry!

64

1950s Sand pail made in England by Happynack along with a Pelham golly puppet and three 1950s golly dolls. Values range from £50/$75to £250/$385.

Robertsons shop display box containing the entire premium golly dolls issued by Robertsons from the 1970s onwards. This set is valued at £100/$150+.

Steiff dolls, designed for The Toy Store, Toledo USA. to celebrate golly's 100th anniversary "Golli G. & Teddy B". was a limited edition of 1500 and made in 1995, he is the first Steiff golly made since 1917, 9inch tall, made of felt, wearing leather boots and carrying a tiny bear. The following year "Miss Molly & Peg" appeared, she was a limited edition of 2500 and the first girl golly ever made by Steiff. She is 9inch tall, made of felt, wearing black leather boots and is holding a small wooden peg doll. These are valued at £150/$220+.

Modern "World of Miniature Bears" golly range.£35/$50 each.

Golly artists and collectors can be found in many countries around the world. And I am so pleased to have in my collection "Golli's Uncle Sam". A lovely collector's item made in America by William H. (Bill) Boyd. An edition of 200 "Uncle Sam" was accompanied by a wonderful short story written by Bill of how Golly came to be. £50-£60/$75-$90.

Selection of miniatures including "Webster" by Sue Wilkes with "Golly on a button" and "Fairy Golly" made by Davina Roberts. Values from £10-£40/$15-$60.

Carlton Ware Gollies

In 1999, Carlton Ware began to make a commemorative issue of the 1970s Golly band they had made for Robertsons. This new set, produced independently of Robertsons, and produced only with the Carlton Ware logo, became and immediate seller. Each item in the band is a different edition size, with those that are sold out commanding a premium on the collectors market. In 2002 they produced other golly items like the golly flying teapot, and a new 'small size' series of gollies which are passionately collected by a growing band of followers. Here we see a gallery of items. In order to 'spread the word' on these and other items, Carlton Ware are selling selected items on ebay and through their own site - carltonware.co.uk. As these items are auctioned, the price is often not specific, and so collectors can pick up a bargain. Very often though, the items sell for more than the retail price, and when trials or prototypes have been put up for sale, they have often fetched three to four times the price of a normal piece. Carlton Ware now deliberately put up 'special' items on ebay on the first of each month, so it is worth looking at the site for these. They are fun to watch out for, even if you can't afford them.

The Large Band Set, commonly referred to as Blow Ups' comprises, in order of appearance:
The Golly Guitar. Limited Edition 250
The Golly Accordion. Limited Edition 1000
The Golly Cello (or Double Bass) Limited Edition 1000
The Golly Singer. Limited Edition 750
The Golly Trumpeter. Limited Edition 500
The Golly Saxophone. Limited Edition 500
The Golly Drummer. Unlimited.
The Golly Clarinet. Limited Edition 250
Mystery Ninth: A Mystery

The quality and size of these items is simply fabulous, and there can be no finer celebration of the Golly world than this fabulous set. It has gone from strength to strength. In order to keep up with peoples pockets, Carlton Ware introduced some smaller gollies in 2002. These were introduced at £25 each and appeared in sets of varying numbers. The first was Set One which comprised a set of eight figures with a mystery ninth. The build up of the sets has been organised so that as they build, subsets will appear. For instance, the band members will appear over a number of sets, the Bride and Groom are in different sets. Sporting Gollies will appear in different sets, as will the Indian Chief and Cowboy etc. For updates it is best to contact Carlton Ware directly on 0208 318 9580.

Set One is made up of:
The Golly Guitar. Limited Edition 450
The Golly King. Limited Edition 450
The Golly Policeman. Limited Edition 350
The Golly Patriot (UK). Limited Edition 450
The Golly Nurse. Limited Edition 350
The Golly Waiter. Limited Edition 350
The Golly Graduate. Limited Edition 350
The Golly Bride. Limited Edition 350
The Mystery Ninth is a mystery

Set Two is made up of:
The SuperGolly
The Golly Queen
The Golly Baker
The Golly Accordion
The Golly King
The Mystery Sixth is a mystery

Set Three is made up of:
Golly Disco Dancer
Golly Magician
Golly Groom
Golly Drummer
Golly Builder
Again, the Mystery Sixth is a mystery

Set Four is made up of:
The Golly Skier
The Golly Artist
The Golly Lover Boy
Big Chief Standing Golly say 'HOW'
The Golly Sax
Again, the mystery Sixth is a mystery

Carlton Ware Gollies

A group of the Carlton Ware Gollies, the flying teapot, the Golly Guitar, and some cuties from the smaller series, which are about 4 inches (10cm) high. This is a good picture for showing the proportions of the gollies. The Golly Guitar now sells for over £150, the Golly flying teapot prototype version has sold for over £200, with individual trials from the first set of gollies fetching over £60 each.

The Golly Cello, or Double Bass. All the larger Band set are an impressive 20cm (9 inches) high.

The bright front-man of the band, full of charm and character

Carlton Ware Gollies

Trial colourway of the Golly Trumpeter. He also has the unusual characteristic of moulded eyebrows and slightly 'boz' eyes as he blows away...

The second Carlton Ware set includes just five members. There is also a mystery sixth, which again is a mystery, so we can't tell you what it is....

The first set of the small size gollies. They vary from 31/2 to 4 inches in height. Issued with certificates, the edition sizes vary slightly. There is also a mystery ninth... Which is a mystery, so we can't tell you what it is....

Carlton Ware Gollies

Set three is a lovely set, as the Gollies are really starting to take hold and the series begins to establish itself. The mystery sixth is a mystery - still...

The golly is getting more and more adventurous. And again there is a mystery firgure.

Golly Figures

Carltonware Bandstand £350-£375/$520-$575; Carltonware Musicians £45-£50/$65-$75 each. All together are worth over £600/$900. Watch out for fakes, which are common. If you see crudely painted musicians with white bases and 'Carlton Ware' in red on the back, they are worthless fakes.

Set of five Wade china golly figures. These were the first golly figures to be issued by Robertson's in the 1960s and are very collectable by both wade and golly collectors. Only five variations are believed to have been issued and because of cost did not last for long, being superseded by chalk ones made in Portugal. £100-£130/$150-$200 each.

Golly Figures

Set of eleven plastic golly football players from the 1960-70s, later to be issued by Robertsons made of chalk. £15/$22 each.

Golly Figures

Childs cardboard play clock, used to teach children to tell the time in 1950s. Maker unknown. £60-£70/$90-$105.

1950s Australian green triangularly candy tin £80/$120 and rubber squeaky toy, £50-£55/$75-$85

Special edition "Colourbox" golly pottery figure designed by Peter Fagan and made around the 1990s. Toy Box £60/$90; Golly £45-£50/$65-$75.

Golly Figures

From the Colour Box String things range he is called "Louis". £50-£70/$75-$105.

Colour Box Razzle Dazzle collection "Lamp post" Limited Edition of 2000. Value £75-£100/$110-$155.

Colour Box Razzle Dazzle collection "Golly Pals". £70-£90/$105-$140.

Golly Figures

A superb hand painted Golly and Teddy made in Shropshire by Eurocraft. £50-£70/$75-$105.

This Golly by Clarice Cliff is a lovely example and is worth about £2000. Courtesy of Bearnes Auction House.

Made in England, this Cloth Tag original was hand crafted and was a limited edition of 5000 in 1995. £50-£60/$75-$90.

Pottery moneybox with the makers name and patent number on the bottom. Made in Stoke on Trent in the early 1960s, he is approximately 6in tall, has a green jacket and holds a blackboard with the words "Let Golly Save Your Lolly", £150/$220+.

10in pottery moneybox, maker unknown but thought to have been made in the 1950s, he has blue jacket, striped trousers and wobbly eyes, £150/$200+.

Pottery moneybox, maker unknown, it comes in various colours and sizes and was made in the 1930s. This one is approx 5inch tall, has a pink collar and wobbly eyes. £120-£160/$180-$215.

A Royal Doulton China Robertson's Golly Advertising Figure, 6" high. £50-£80/$75-$120.

Four of the set of six golly trinket boxes made in 1970-80s by Dodo Designs, they depict gollies playing musical instruments and there are two of each colour; yellow, red and blue. £50-£55/$75-$85 each.

Four more Robertsons Golly plastic Trinket Boxes by Dodo Designs.

Golly Pottery

Robertsons Golly Pottery list and price guide

Cheesedish Skier	£600-£650
Carltonware Teapot Golly/Squares	£450-£475
Butterdish Table Tennis	£450-£475
Sugar Bowl Golly Playing Piano	£375-£395
Toby Jug	£375-£395
Ceramic Money Box	£375-£395
Carlton Bandstand	£350-£375
Cricket Teapot	£325-£350
Standard Teapot	£275-£295
Milk Jug	£275-£295
Salt and Pepper Musicians	£225-£250
Salt and Pepper Squares	£225-£250

Red Rim Breakfast Set

Cereal Bowl	£50- £55
Plate	£50-£55
Mug	£50-£55
Eggcup	£50-£55

Yellow Rim Breakfast Set

Cereal Bowl	£40-£45
Plate	£40-£45
Mug	£40-£45
Eggcup	£20-£25

Drummer Eggcup	£45
Sailing Club	£45
Plastic Head and Shoulders Golly Eggcup	£30-£35
Boxed Set of two H/Shoulders Golly Eggcups	£80-£85

Toastracks

Gollytimes/Toast	£30-£35
Motorcyclist	£30-£35
Golly Holding Jar	£40-£45

Mugs
Set of Nine

Bass Player	Cricket Player	Drummer	
Footballer	Golfer	Guitarist	
Standard Golly	Tennis Player	Tuba Player	£60-£65 Each

Set of Six

American	Cricketer	Footballer	
Golfer	Skateboarder	Tennis Player	£60-£65 Each

Easter Mug	£20-£25
Jolly Golly	£35-£40
Several Gollies	£20-£25
Thank Golly Its Friday	£20-£25

Musicians

Wade	£110-£130 each
Carltonware	£45-£50 each
Pottery	£10 each
Footballers	£15 each
Lollipop/School Crossing	£15

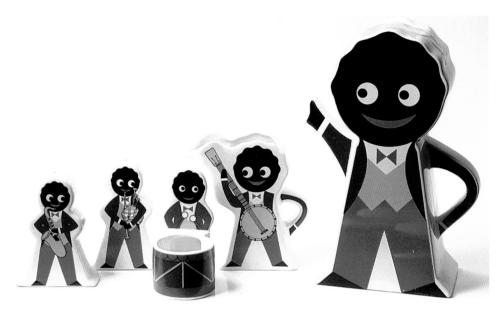

1980s Silver Crane china made under license from Robertson's Teapot, milk jug, egg cup and salt & pepper shakers are all highly sought after by golly collectors. Salt and Peppers Musicians, £225-£250/$335-$370; Drummer Eggcup £45/$65; Milk Jug £275-£295/$405-$450; Standard Golly Teapot £250-£295/$370-$450

Mugs £60-£65/$90-$100; Drummer eggcup £45/$65; Cricket Teapot £325-£350/$480-$535.

Left to right: Very rare china moneybox issued by James Robertson and sons in the 1980s. Robertson's golly tankard 1980s with two miniature soft golly dolls and the golly from the Royal Doulton Millennium issue of advertising figurines. Ceramic Moneybank £350-£395/$520-$605; Golly Doll £25-£28/$35-$43; Christmas Golly £30-£35/$45-$55; Silver Edged mug £125-£150/$185-$230. Royal Doulton Golly from the Millennium set of eight 20th century Classics, limited edition of 2000, £300-£350/$445-$535.

Robertsons China Salt and Pepper pots. Made by the Silver Crane Co.£225-£250/$335-$385.

Robertsons China Butter Dish £450-£475/$665-$725.

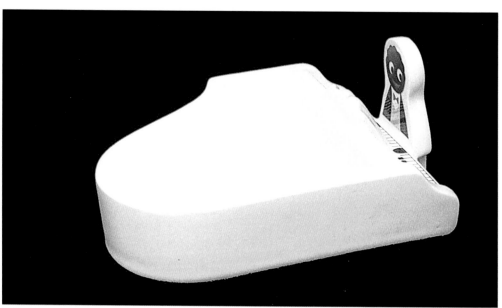

Golly Piano Sugar Bowl, made by Silver Crane Co. £375-£395/$555-$605.

Group of Mable Lucy Attwell nursery ware made by Shelley and showing golly and "Boo Boo", they are highly sought after by both Mable Lucy Attwell and golly collectors. £295-£325/$435-$495.

Baby's feeding dish showing golly and children by unknown maker thought to have been made around the 1920s. £110/$165.

German china tea set made by Koenigszelt, decorated in an art deco style and made around the 1930s. Golly Trio, Plate, Cup and Saucer, £225-£250/$335-$385.

Toastrack Golly Times/Toast £30-£35/$45-$55.

Selection of nursery ware made by Swinnertons in the 1930s. This pattern was also used by Empire ware, it is known as Gollywog Sports and depicts golly in amusing sports situations with Comical captions. Plate/Dish £110/$165; Plate £100-£125/$150-$190; Cup £65-£75/$95-$115; Plate/Dish £110/$165.

Quite a few of the potteries in England produced children's china depicting golly, here is a selection dating from the 1900s to 1960s and ranging from babies dishes to full services. Mug £55-£60/$80-$90; Plate £125-£145/$185-$215; Beaker £60-£75/$90-$115; Plate, Cup and Saucer trio £225/$335.

Joan Allen Plates

These plates are included as collectable plates, handpainted by Joan Allen. Very little is known of her, but these cute paintings heavily feature the Golly and are included here. Small items fetch £100-£150, medium size items £150-£250 and large size items £250-£400 on the collectors market. All are naively, but nevertheless fetchingly handpainted on white ware. Trade marks on the base are purely coincidental and are nothing to do with the manufacturer.

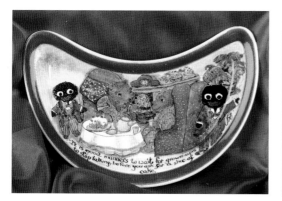

Joan Allen Plates

Joan Allen Plates

Robertsons Golly Brooches and Badges

No Golly book would be complete without the addition of Robertsons Golly Brooches/Badges. This is a vast area of collecting with makers, variations and colourways all determining prices.

Following is a list of Golly brooches as they were introduced by Robertsons. We also have photographs of many of the brooches. Finally, we have incorporated some values for the general reader. Colin Dodds work on listing variations is second to none, and we would advise the avid collector to go to his book. However, Ebay has become a very important source for Golly brooches. Following our listing is an approximate price guide to Robertson's badges, based on sales on Ebay, and other Internet sites.

1920
Bakelite Golly
Tin Badge with Leather Hat
Tin With Hair

1928
Jolly Golly Golfer

1932
Pre-war Fruits
Blackcurrant
Bramble
Lemon
Orange
Raspberry
Strawberry

1935-1939
Union Jack Waistcoat Coronation Golly
Enamels with Yellow 'Golden Shred' Waistcoats
Tennis Golly
Hockey Golly
Footballers
Cricketers
Club Cricketers

1950s-1960s

Enamels with White 'Golden Shred' Waistcoat

Bagpiper
Cricketer
Footballer
Golfer
Guitarist
Hockey
Lollipopman
Scout
Skater
Standard
Tennis Player

Fruits

Lemon
Raspberry

1960s Pro-Pat Designs

Skater
Standard

1970s

Enamels with Yellow Waistcoat

Bagpiper
Cricketer
Footballer
Golfer
Guitarist
Hockey
Lollipopman
Motorcyclist
Scout
Skater
Skateboarder
Standard
Tennis Player

1980s Acrylics (pointed feet)

Ambulanceman
American Footballer
Astronaut
Bagpiper

Baker Viota
Brownie
Butcher
Car Driver
Commemerative 1930-1980
Cowboy
Cricketer
Cyclist
Darts Player
Doctor
Engine Driver
Fireman
Fisherman
Footballer
Golfer
Guitarist
Jogger
Lollipopman
Milkman
Motorcyclist
Mountie
Nurse
Policeman
Postman
Racing Car Driver No. 23
Sailor
Skier
Snooker Player
Standard
Tennis Player

1980s Acrylics Fruits (Bubble Coated)
Orange
Lemon
Strawberry
Raspberry
Blackcurrant

1980s Special Promotions
Bank It
Cystic Fibrosis Limited Edition of 2000
HMS Crichton

Golly Club
Lifeboatman
Viota Baker in 9carat Gold
Viota Baker Silver
Viota Baker with 'Diamond' in Spoon
Fireman Nozzle in Silver

Mid 1980s Collectors Enamels
Oranges with Scroll Limited Edition
Lemons with Scroll Limited Edition

1985
'1940s Boxed Set' Enamels, Set of White Waistcoat Reproductions
Standard
Footballer
Golfer
Guitarist
Hockey
Tennis

1990s Acrylics (smaller eyes rounded feet)
American Footballer
Astronaut
Baseball Player
Brownie
Cricketer
Doctor
Fireman
Fisherman
Footballer
Jockey
Juggler
Keep Fit
McGolly
Nurse
Policeman
Racing Driver No.1
Skateboarder
Skier
Standard
Surfer
Tennis Player

Father Christmas {Promotion sor staff only, Limited Edition of 2400}

1992
Olympic Special Limited Edition Set of four
A 6mm bar at the bottom of each Brooch says Barcelona 92
Discus
Gymnast
Hurdler
Torch Bearer

1994
New Golly Collectors Club

1993-1996 Large Acrylics
Air Hostess
Australian
Ballet Dancer
Chef
Cyclist
Footballer
French Golly
Juggler
Karate
Keep Fit
McGolly
Nurse
Pilot
Policeman
Racing Driver
Rugby Player
Skier
Standard
Surfer
Swimmer
Walker

1996
Limited Edition set of five brooches:
Baby
Clown
Flamenco Dancer
Mountie

Pirate
Range of Ten
Artist
Cheerleader
DIY
Eskimo
Ice Hockey
Knight
Paperboy
Scarecrow
Viking
Wren

1998
World Cup Golly, boxed limited edtion of 5000
Santa/Rudolph boxed Cloisonne Golly Brooch special edition
Set of Nine
Basketball
Doctor
Goalkeeper
Golfer
Guitarist
Judge
Saxophonist
Singer
Waiter

1999
Set of Twelve
Bride
Brownie
Caveman
Graduate
Groom
King
Mermaid
Queen
Roman
Scout
Wizard
Classic Year 2000 (Millennium)

2000

Farmer

Euro 2000 Set

Belgium

Denmark

England

Germany

Holland

Italy

Silver Millennium boxed Golly Brooch, Limited edition 2000

Paisley Exhibition Badge

Gollympic Games 2000 Limited Edition 2000 boxed sets

Equestrian

Hurdler

Rower

Shot Putter

Weightlifter

2001

Golly Diary 2001 - 3000 boxed sets issued Days of the Week

Historical Events from the 20th Century set of ten

1900	1903 Wright Brothers
1910	1912 Total Eclipse
1920	1922 Tutankhamun's Tomb discovered
1930	1932 London Philharmonic Orchestra founded
1940	1946 First casual shirt
1950	1953 Structure of DNA
1960	1969 Woodstock
1970	1970 Spacehoppers
1980	1981 First London Marathon
1990	1993 The Grand National was abandonded

Farewell Golden Golly Badge 9ct Gold boxed 5000 issued

2002

Silver Farewell Golly Badge 3000 issued

Balloon Badges

Golly II and III Both Balloons Together Bronze Metal

Golly II and III Both Balloons Together Silver Metal

Golly III 1998 Golly III ... Alburquerque 1998

Golly Balloon Balloon I Silver Finish White Basket Red Bow Tie

4 Golly Balloons Quadruple Balloon Golly I to IV Judith B/S

Golly I G-Bbbt Circular-White Background

Golly II Bdfg Circular-White Background

Golly III G-Olli Circular - White Background

Golly IV G-Ollie Circular- White Background

Golly III 1995 Rectangle With Golly III Tours 24 June 1995

Castle Howard Castle Howard, York

Balloon 1977 Golly II

Golly Badges

The most desirable of all the golly brooches has to be the pre-wars. There were several designs issued starting with a golly golfer and including; a set of six fruits brooches with tiny golly heads, a 1937 Brooch issued to celebrate the Coronation, a set of county cricketers and football players with different coloured balls. With a few exceptions all the brooches were made by Miller and had the patent number on the reverse. They can be identified by their Yellow waistcoats and "Golden Shred" on their chests. Pre-war Fruits can be worth as much as £500 each, and the pre-war Golden Shred badges also fetch a premium. See price guide

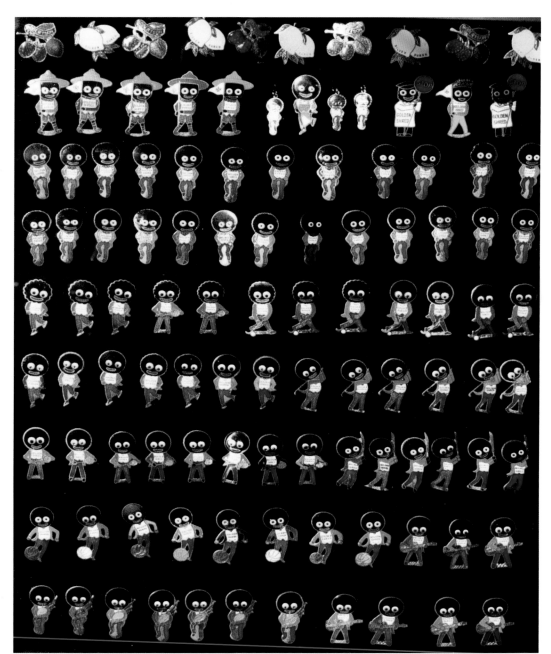

Golly enamel brooches issued by Robertsons in the 1950-60s, they can be recognised by their white waistcoats with "Golden Shred" across the chest. This was Robertson's most popular period, other manufacturers had to be employed to cope with the demand, some only made small quantities and their brooches are now eagerly sought by collectors. Most can be obtained between £5-£30 with a few exceptions.

Golly Badges

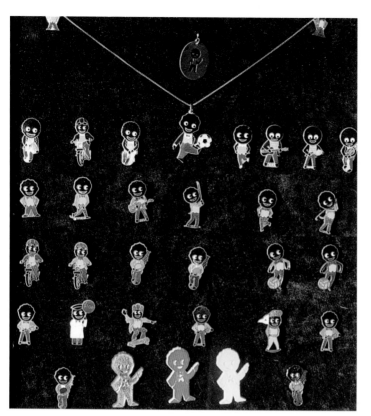

In 1970 Robertsons changed the design of their enamel brooches, they were of poorer quality, the waistcoat was changed back to yellow and the words "Golden Shred" were removed. Only a few makers were involved in the manufacture of these brooches; Gomm, Fattorini and Coffer.

The Badges produced in the 1970's had plain yellow waistcoats and eyes that looked to the right. There were 13 badges in all. The Scout and the Cricketer are not shown in the photograph. The tin button badges (still commonly found today) and the standard pendant shown are also from the same era.

Golly Badges

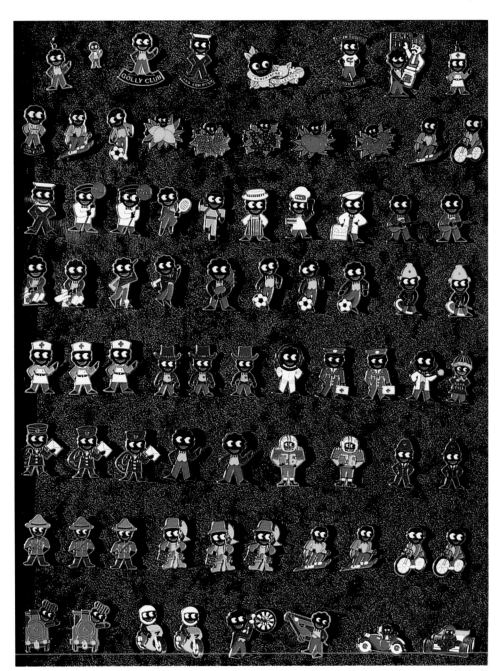

The very first issue of acrylic golly brooches issued by Robertson's in the 1980s along with some rarer limited edition brooches including; HMS Crichton, issued to crew members when Robertsons adopted their ship; Cystic Fibrosis, issued to help raise money for the Cystic Fibrosis charity; Golly Club, issued by Robertson's in 1985 to members of the newly formed and short lived golly club

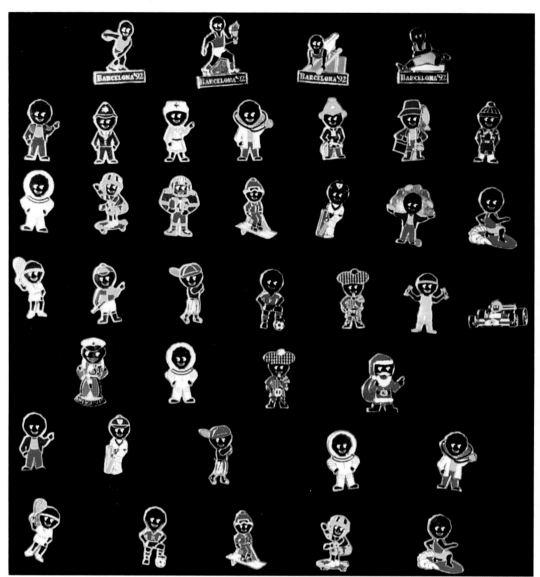

Set of acrylic golly brooches issued by Robertsons in 1990 when you could send off three tokens and 50p to obtain one. Also included is the special limited edition set of four brooches issued to celebrate the 1992 Olympics in Barcelona.

Collection of Robertson's 1993/94 acrylic golly brooches. These brooches were much larger than previous and had a bubble coating on top. Two sets were produced and can be identified by the back stamp which is horizontal on the 1993 set and vertical on the 1994.

Golly Badges

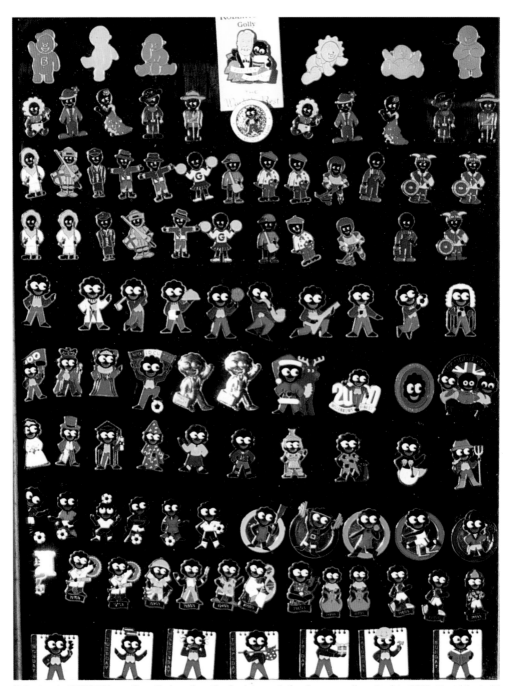

Robertson's 1999/2001 acrylic golly brooches, the final issues before he was sadly retired in 2001. To celebrate his retirement Robertsons invited collectors to purchase a gold and silver farewell brooch.

Golly Badges

A selection of tin brooches and key rings issued by Robertsons over the years.

A collection of golly balloon brooches, stickers and postcards. Most were not issued by Robertsons but made for balloon enthusiasts and sold at balloon festivals.

Golly Badges

A selection of Robertson's badges from the 1950's and 1960's. including the Raspberry and Lemon fruits.

A further selection of badges from the 1980's including a commemorative tin button badge "50 GOLDEN YEARS".

Golly Badges

The selection of 1980's badges includes the strawberry and orange fruits, which have reached £90.00 each at auction recently.

A Gold farewell Golly brooch was issued to coincide with the announcement of Golly's retirement in August 2001. Only 5000 were made and were available only to "lifetime collectors" at a cost £25.00 and had to be ordered on a special application form. It became clear that there was a huge demand for a farewell tribute by those collectors who missed out on the Gold brooch, so a Silver Farewell badge was produced. Identical to the Gold version it came in a similar presentation box with a certificate but it was only limited to one per household and cost £15.00.

Golly Badges

Golly's Diary 2001 comprising of seven badges in a presentation gift box was priced at £25.00. On the Inside of the box was printed the rhyme: Monday's Golly is fair of face, Tuesday's Golly is full of grace,Wednesday's Golly is full of woe, Thursday's Golly has far to go, Friday's Golly is loving and giving,Saturday's Golly works hard for a living, But the Golly who is born on the Sabbath day, Is fair and wise and good and gay. Golly's Diary set has recently been sold for £150.00 at auction.

The Father Christmas cloisonné badge issued in 1998 was a special edition of 10,000 and came presented in a green velour presentation box with the words. Have a Jolly Golly Christmas printed on the inside of the lid in gold lettering. Each was sequentially numbered and cost £7.00. Only one badge per household could be ordered. This has reached £157.00 at auction. The World Cup Golly Brooch issued the same year was limited to 5,000 again sequentially numbered and presented in a black velour box with Golly it's Good! Printed on the inside of the lid in gold lettering. It cost just £5.00 but has recently sold for over £80.00 at auction.

Golly Badges

Olympic set of four badges featuring Discus, Gymnast, Hurdler and the Torchbearer.

The Great Golly Giveaway badge, a limited edition of 500 was produced for Children in need 2001. When applying, collectors were asked to donate a Golly item for auction. A hallmarked silver version approved by Robertson's was available for £45.00 in 2002 with all proceeds going to Children in need. A limited edition of 250 it sold out immediately.

The Historical Events From the 20th Century. A set of 10 badges depicting various events that took place over the years: 1903-Wright Brothers took their first flight; 1912-Total Eclipse of the Sun was visible; 1922-Tomb of Tutankhamen discovered; 1932-The London Philharmonic Orchestra was founded; 1946- the first casual shirt was adopted which was the Hawaiian shirt; 1953-Structure of DNA discovered; 1969-400,000 people attended the Woodstock Festival; 1970-Spacehopper was born; 1981-First London Marathon was run with 7055 competitors; 1993-Grand National was abandoned after two false starts

Golly Badges

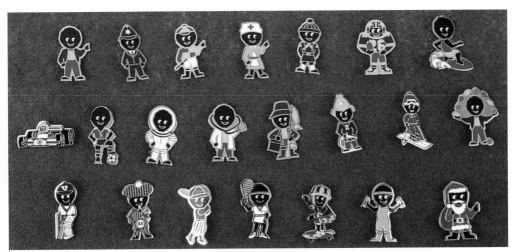

A 1990's set of 21 Acrylic Badges. Standard, Policeman, Jockey, Nurse, Brownie, American Footballer, Surfer, Racing Driver No 1, Footballer, Astronaut, Doctor, Fisherman, Fireman, Skier, Juggler, Cricketer, McGolly, Baseball Player, Tennis Player, Skateboarder, and Keep Fit. The Father Christmas badge was a Staff Promotion with only 2400 being made.

The 1998 Range of 10 consist of a Guitarist, Saxophonist, Singer, Basketball player, Waiter, Judge, Standard, Golfer, Doctor and Goal keeper.

Golly Badges

The 1999 Range of 12 Badges include a King, Queen, Groom, Bride, Caveman, Wizard, Millennium Classic, Mermaid, Roman, Brownie, Scout and Graduate. The Farmer was issued separately, promoted only on jars of organic mincemeat in 2000.

The Bubble Coated Clown, Pirate, Baby, Mountie and Flamenco Golly were a Limited Edition available between 31st of May and the 1st of November 1996. The Baby alone has sold for £88.00. The other badges shown were issued from November and featured a DIY, Artist, Scarecrow, Wren, Ice Hockey, Viking, Eskimo, Cheerleader, Paperboy and Knight

Golly Internet Sales

Prices achieved during 2002 via the Internet. All are Robertsons badges unless otherwise stated. The description column is that given by the seller and is not necessarily accurate.

Name	Date	Series	GB£	US$	Description
1900s Golly		Historic Events	£3.20	$4.88	
1900s Golly		Historic Events	£2.21		
1900s Golly		Historic Events	£2.41		
1900s Golly		Historic Events	£4.44		
1910s Golly		Historic Events	£2.20		
1910s Golly		Historic Events	£3.70		
1910s Golly		Historic Events	£3.31		
1920s Golly		Historic Events	£2.01		
1920s Golly		Historic Events	£2.21		
1920s Golly		Historic Events	£3.20		
1930s Golly		Historic Events	£3.00	$4.57	
1930s Golly		Historic Events	£3.17		
1930s Golly		Historic Events	£3.79		
1930s Golly		Historic Events	£3.89		
1940s Golly		Historic Events	£1.45		
1940s Golly		Historic Events	£2.20		
1940s Golly		Historic Events	£3.89		
1940s Golly	1985	Historic Events	£63.11	133.30	
1950s Golly		Historic Events	£1.20		
1950s Golly		Historic Events	£2.40		
1950s Golly		Historic Events	£2.75		
1990s Golly		Historic Events	£4.20		
1950s Golly		Historic Events	£4.13		
1960s Golly		Historic Events	£1.99		
1960s Golly		Historic Events	£4.48		
1960s Golly		Historic Events	£3.54		
1970s Golly		Historic Events	£3.39		
1970s Golly		Historic Events	£3.76		
1970s Golly		Historic Events	£4.95		
1980s Golly		Historic Events	£2.01		
1980s Golly		Historic Events	£3.89		
1990s Golly		Historic Events	£1.81		
1990s Golly		Historic Events	£3.19		
1990s Golly		Historic Events	£4.31		
Accordian			£5.00	$7.72	
Advertising Golly			£156.10	$241.02	Large
Aerobics/Keep Fit				$17.50	
Air Hostess	1993/6		£7.50		
Air Hostess	1993/6		£9.50		
Air Hostess			£4.00		
Air Hostess			£4.99	$7.61	
Ambulanceman			£38.30	$58.38	
Ambulanceman	1980s		£31.04	$47.93	
American Footballer			£4.95	$7.64	
American Footballer			£10.50	$16.01	

Name	Date	Series	GB£	US$	Description
American Footballer			£4.99	$7.61	
American Footballer			£5.70		Mint
American Footballer	1990		£7.00		
American Footballer			£4.70		
American Footballer			£4.42		
American Footballer			£5.50	$8.49	Colourway
Angler	1990s		£5.01		
Angler			£5.50		Mint
Artist	1996		£4.31		
Artist	1996		£4.70		
Artist	1996			$6.50	
Artist	1996		£5.50	$8.49	
Artist			£4.63	$7.06	
Artist			£4.00	$6.18	
Astronaut	1980s		£5.00	$7.72	
Astronaut			£5.50	$8.38	
Astronaut	1980s		£4.70		
Astronaut	1980s		£4.90		
Astronaut	1990s		£6.51	$10.05	Mint in bag
Astronaut	1980s		£285		Blue, enamel missing from both eyes
Astronaut			£92.50		Unusual
Astronaut			£84.65		Eyes facing right
Australian	1993/6		£5.10		
Australian			£16.00	$24.70	Yellowy Hat
Australian			£9.52	$14.70	Darker Hat
Australian			£10.50	$16.01	
Australian			£3.50		
Australian			£4.20		
Australian				$5.00	Large
Australian	1993/94			$6.50	Large
Baby Set			£156.00		Comprises: Baby, Clown, Flamenco Dancer Mountie, Pirate
Baby Set			£200.00		Comprises: Baby, Clown, Flamenco Dancer Mountie, Pirate
Baby Set			£186.35		Comprises: Baby, Clown, Flamenco Dancer Mountie, Pirate
Bagpiper			£28.01	$43.25	
Bagpiper	1960s		£20.13	$31.08	Gomm
Bagpiper			£115.55	$176.13	Green Bag, White Waistcoat, H W Miller
Bagpiper			£57.00		Big eyes
Bagpiper			£9.99	$15.23	
Bagpiper			£14.00		W/W
Bagpiper	1980s		£138.26	$213.47	Mint in Bag
Baker			£8.00	$12.35	
Baker			£31.50	$48.02	Viota
Baker	1980		£30.00		Viota
Baker			£40.00	$60.97	Viota
Baker	1980			$45.00	Viota
Baker	1980s		£25.00		Viota
Baker	1980s		£31.00		Viota
Baker	1980s		£33.51		Viota
Baker	1980s		£29.20		Viota
Ballerina			£2.95	$4.55	
Ballerina			£5.60	$8.65	
Ballerina			£4.20		
Ballerina				$6.00	Large
Ballet Dancer			£5.00	$7.72	
Ballet Dancer			£5.51	$8.40	
Balloon Golly III			£15.00	$23.16	
Balloon			£10.51	$16.02	

Name	Date	Series	GB£	US$	Description
Balloon			£16.00	$24.39	50 Great Golly Giveaway III Balloon Pin Badge
Band Master			£10.50	$16.21	
Band Players			£16.25	$25.09	
Bandstand Voucher	1980s		£4.00	$6.18	
Bank It	1980s		£104.20		
Bank It	1980s		£225.00		Very rare
Bank It	1980s		£325.00		
Barcellona 1992			£75.00		Games Set
Baseball	1990		£5.00	$7.62	
Baseball	1990s		£3.12		
Baseball			£4.20	$6.48	
Basketballer			£3.72	$5.67	
Bike			£4.99		
Bi-Plane			£3.70	$5.71	1900 on it
Blackcurrant			£112		Face among blackcurrants, damaged
Blackcurrant	Pre-war		£500		
Bookmark				$8.00	Rare, Mint
Bramble	Pre-War		£180.00		Slight damage
Bride Doll			£10.02	$15.47	
Brown Patch Guide			£16.00		
Brownie			£3.70	$5.64	
Brownie			£6.50		Mint
Brownie	1990		£7.00		
Brownie			£3.50		
Brownie			£4.00		Big Eyes
Brownie	1980			$8.00	
Brownie	1980s		£5.00	$7.72	
Butcher			£34.01		Impressed James Robertson, size 30mm
Butcher			£37.00	$56.40	Blue Apron, White Hat
Butcher	1980		£34.00		Nice
Butcher	1980s			$19.99	
Butcher	1980			$45.00	
Butcher	1980		£33.06		
Button				$4.50	
Button (Set of 4)			£15.00		
Buy Me				$9.99	Rare
Car Driver			£9.01		
Car Driver	1980s		£13.00	$20.07	
Caveman	1999		£5.01		MIB
Caveman	1990		£4.20	$6.48	
Cheerleader	1996		£4.11		
Cheerleader	1996		£4.70		
Cheerleader	1996			$6.50	
Chef			£10.50	$16.21	
Chef	1993/94			$6.95	Large
Chef			£9.00		
Chef				AU$30.00	
Chef				$5.00	Large Thin
Chef			£4.99		
Chef	1993-6		£6.51		
Clarinet Player Figure			£10.50	$16.21	
Clarinet Player Figure			£8.00	$12.35	
Classic Pose			£4.99		
Commemorative			£42.05	$64.10	

Name	Date	Series	GB£	US$	Description
Cowboy			£3.50	$5.34	
Cowboy			£4.20	$6.40	
Cowboy			£5.53		
Cowboy	1980			$8.00	
Cowboy	1980		£7.00		
Cowboy	1980s		£5.00	$7.62	
Cricketer			£10.00	$15.24	Lancs
Cricketer				$316.00	H W Miller, Golden Shred, Lancs
Cricketer			£15.00	$22.86	Northants
Cricketer			£12.75	$19.69	
Cricketer			£10.50	$16.21	
Cricketer			£18.00	$27.44	New Zealand
Cricketer			£4.99		
Cricketer			£5.19		
Cricketer			£6.05		Middlesex
Cricketer			£7.02		Surrey
Cricketer	Pre War		£200		Surrey
Cricketer			£7.51		Durham
Cricketer			£9.00	$13.72	Sussex
Cricketer	Pre War		£175.00		Essex
Cricketer	Pre War		£90.00		Essex
Cricketer			£10.00	$15.24	Golden Shred
Cricketer			£12.75	$19.43	
Cricketer			£21.00		W/W
Cricketer	1980s		£141.00	$217.70	
Cricketer	1980s		£77.00		In orginal packet
Cricketer	1980			$90.00	Small bat
Cricketer	Pre War		£149.99	$228.63	MOC
Cyclist			£12.50	$19.30	
Cyclist	1980s		£13.50	$20.84	
Cyclist			£10.51		
Cyclist			£4.20		
Cyclist			£5.00		
Cyclist			£5.50	$8.38	
Cyclist			£7.51	$11.45	
Cyclist	1980s		£16.00	$24.39	Bubble Coated
Cyclist	1980s		£9.00	$13.72	Flat Finish
Cyclist	1980s		£10.50	$16.01	Bubble finish
Cyclist	1980s		£15.00		Bubble Coated
Cyclist			£9.03		
Cyclist				$5.70	Large
Cyclist			£10.50		Bubble
Cyclist	1980			$22.00	Bubble
Cyclist	1980			$22.00	Flat
Cyclist	1980		£14.49		
Cyclist	1980s		£8.50	$13.12	
Darts Player			£15.47		
Darts Player	1980			$42.00	
DIY	1996			$6.50	
DIY	1996		£3.70		
DIY	1996		£4.20		
Doctor	1998		£3.92		
Doctor			£7.50	$11.58	
Doctor			£10.00	$15.24	
Doctor			£4.10		
Doctor			£4.21	$6.42	
Doctor			£4.99		
Doctor	1990s		£3.00		
Doctor	1980s		£4.00		
Doctor	1980s		£6.50		
Doctor	1980s		£5.00	$7.72	
Double Balloon			£20.02	$30.52	

Name	Date	Series	GB£	US$	Description
Double Balloon			£10.55		Gilt Mint
Double Balloon			£15.00	$22.86	
Double Balloon			£16.01	$24.40	
Double Balloon			£23.00	$35.06	
Double Balloon			£34.00	$51.83	
Double Balloon			£12.50		
Double Balloon			£8.50		
Double Bass Player Figure			£6.00	$9.26	
Drummer Figure			£5.50	$8.49	
England Badge + 1966 Stamp			£12.00		
England Football			£8.05	$12.27	
Eskimo	1996		£4.41		
Eskimo	1996			$5.70	
Eskimo			£6.76	$10.30	
Eskimo			£5.50	$8.49	
Farewell Golly			£122.00	$185.96	Gold Enamel, Brooch clasp, only 100 made
Farewell Golly			£72.00	$109.75	Gold Enamel
Farewell Golly			£20.00		Enamel -Silver
Farewell Golly				$30.00	Silver
Farewell Golly			£31.00		Silver
Farmer				$8.37	
Father Christmas	1998		£28.50	$44.00	
Father Christmas	1998		£29.00	$44.78	
Fireman	1980s		£5.50	$8.38	Long Hose
Fireman			£4.95	$7.64	
Fireman	1980s		£10.51	$16.23	
Fireman			£4.00		
Fireman			£6.50	$9.91	
Fireman	Early			$9.99	
Fireman			£7.71		
Fireman	1990s		£5.57		
Fireman			£4.20		
Fireman			£4.99	$7.61	
Fireman			£5.50	$8.38	
Fireman			£7.50	$11.43	
Fireman	1990		£4.00	$6.18	
Fisherman			£6.00	$9.26	
Fisherman	1990s		£5.50	$8.49	
Fisherman			£3.50	$5.34	
Fisherman			£4.99		
Fisherman			£4.39	$6.69	
Fisherman			£4.99	$7.61	
Fisherman	1980		£7.00		
Fisherman	1990s		£4.00		
Football Player	1970		£16.00		Gomm
Footballer			£12.50	$19.05	Gomm
Footballer			£15.75	$24.32	
Footballer			£14.50	$22.39	Mint in bag
Footballer			£18.90		
Footballer			£4.99		
Footballer	1980s		£16.05	$24.47	
Footballer	1980s		£32.51	$49.55	Pointed Boot
Footballer	1980s		£8.01		Black Boot
Footballer	Pre-war		£77.13	$117.57	Melsom, Yellow Waistcoat, Blue and White Football
Footballer	Pre-war		£62.00	$94.51	Melsom
Footballer	Pre-war		£4.60		
Footballer			£22.00		
Footballer				$5.50	Large
Footballer			£11.50		W/W
Footballer				$61.56	Black point

Name	Date	Series	GB£	US$	Description
Footballer			£15.75	$24.01	
Footballer			£4.99	$7.61	
Footballer	1980			$55.00	White Boot
Footballer			£7.00	$10.81	
Footballer	1990		£4.00	$6.18	
Footballer			£10.50	$16.21	
Formula 1 Car			£4.99		
Formula 1 Car			£4.99	$7.61	
Formula 1 Car			£5.52	$8.41	
Frenchman			£10.50	$16.21	Large
Frenchman			£3.70		
Frenchman			£5.92	$9.02	
Frenchman			£5.92	$9.14	
Frenchman				$5.00	Large
Frenchman			£4.00		
Frenchman			£5.00		
Fruit			£89.87	$136.99	Rare
Fruit Set	1981		£386.99		Including offer leaflet
Goalkeeper	1998		£3.50		
Goalkeeper			£3.72	$5.67	
Golden Jubilee			£27.01		Ltd Edn 100
Golden Shred			£1.00	$1.54	
Golden Shred			£19.60	$30.26	
Golden Shred			£2.00	$3.09	
Golden Shred	Old		£2.95		
Golden Shred			£1.48	$2.26	
Golden Shred			£1.88	$2.80	
Golden Shred			£19.60	$29.88	
Golden Shred			£2.00	$3.05	
Golden Shred			£2.72		
Golden Shred			£26.55		
Golden Shred			£9.70		
Golden Shred	1980s		£1.70	$2.59	
Golden Shred			£1.88	$2.90	
Golden Shred			£24.60	$37.50	Fattorini
Golden Shred				$72.00	
Golden Shred Tea Towel			£3.92	$6.05	
Golfer	1998		£4.20		
Golfer			£10.51	$16.23	Mint in bag
Golfer			£11.03	$16.81	
Golfer			£2.99	$4.56	
Golfer			£35.25	$53.73	
Golfer			£36.00		
Golfer			£39.50	$60.20	
Golfer			£4.99		
Golfer			£8.00		
Golfer			£8.49		With Yellow Jumper
Golfer	1927		£13.50		
Golfer	1927		£12.50		
Golfer	Old			$15.50	
Golfer			£22.00		Fattorini, White Ball
Golfer			£10.51		
Golfer			£11.01		
Golfer			£14.00		W/W.
Golfer			£29.00		
Golfer				$14.60	
Gollicrush				$30.00	V Rare
Golly Badge& Marmalade Mug			£17.00		
Golly Badge	2002	Commonwealth Games	£15.00		
Golly Club Badge	1980s		£360.00		Rare, with farewell letter etc
Golly Collectors			£570.00	$868.85	

Name	Date	Series	GB£	US$	Description
Golly Easter Mug			£12.50	$19.30	
Golly in Yacht Cloth Badge			£8.19		
Golly Jam Mug/Cup			£17.50	$27.02	
Golly Leaflets x3			£14.50	$22.39	
Golly Offer Leaflets			£4.20	$6.48	
Golly Offers Leaflet	1990		£3.00	$4.63	Cricket
Golly Offers Leaflet	1985		£4.30	$6.64	Squares
Golly Offers Leaflet	1993		£3.00	$4.63	Jet
Golly Offers Leaflet	1993		£4.30	$6.64	Jet
Golly on Bike			£6.51		
Golly on Bike			£8.01		
Golly Pocket Calender	1959		£5.51	$8.51	
Golly Poster			£5.00	$7.72	
Golly Trio Game				$30.00	
Golly With Microphone			£5.00	$7.72	
Golly Paint Book				$5.50	
Golly Diary	2001		£45		3000 boxed sets issued
Goodbye Golly	1928-2001		£21.01	$32.03	Mint in box
Goodbye Golly	1928-2001		£27.00	$41.16	
Goodbye Golly	1928-2001		£27.00	$41.16	Mint
Goodbye Golly	1928-2001		£29.00	$44.20	Limited Edition
Goodbye Golly	1928-2001		£31.00	$47.25	Ltd Edition
Graduate				$9.99	
Graduate	1999		£5.50		
Graduate				$13.00	Mint
Guitar Player	1998		£4.35		
Guitar			£18.21		
Guitar			£6.50		Enamel Stud Back
Guitar			£49.99	$77.18	Fattori,Rare
Guitar	1980			$30.00	
Guitarist			£8.52	$13.15	
Guitarist Figure			£5.00	$7.72	
Guitarist			£4.20	$6.48	
Guitarist	1980s		£3.99	$6.16	
Guitarist			£5.69	$8.79	
Guitarist			£7.09	$10.95	
Guitarist				$24.99	
Guitarist			£22.55		
Guitarist			£3.72	$5.67	
Guitarist			£5.50	$8.38	
Guitarist	50s/60s		£13.50		Mint
Guitarist	50s/60s		£4.99		Mint
Guitarist			£10.00	$15.24	Golden Shred
Guitarist			£10.50	$16.01	Golden Shred
Guitarist			£8.52	$12.99	
Guitarist			£12.51		
Guitarist	1970s		£16.00		
Guitarist	1980s		£37.00	$57.13	
Guitarist			£9.51	$14.68	
Gymnast	1992	Barcelona	£17.01	$25.93	
Gymnast	1992	Barcelona	£16.00	$24.70	
Hawaiin			£3.00	$4.63	1940 on it
Hiker			£13.59	$20.98	Stripey Boots
Hiker			£16.00	$24.70	Green Boots
Hiker			£4.20		
Historic Moments Set			£30.00		
Historic Moments Set			£25.01	$38.62	
Historic Moments Set			£3.00	$4.57	
Historic Moments Set				$125.00	Mint in box
HMS Crichton			£1070.00	$1631.00	Thought, only 50 made.
Hockey Player	1950/1960s		£20.00		

Name	Date	Series	GB£	US$	Description
Hockey Player			£10	$13.50	
Hockey Player			£41.99	$64.01	Curly Hair, White Waistcoat, H W Miller
Hockey Player			£16.50		W/W
Hockey Player			£6.60	$10.19	
Hockey Player			£4.99		
Hockey Player			£12.00	$18.29	
Hockey Player			£14.50		Old Enamel
Hockey Player				$787	H W Miller Ltd, Birmingham
Hurdler	1992	Barcelona	£16.05	$24.47	
Ice Hockey	1996		£4.32		
Ice Hockey	1996		£6.06		
Ice Hockey	1996			$5.70	
Ice Skater	Old		£17.55		
Ice Skater				$15.50	Rare
Ice Skater			£10.00		
I'm A Golly Collector			£23.90		
I've Joined The Golly Club			£10.75	$16.60	
Jam Label	1980		£2.90		
Jet Pilot			£6.50		
Jockey			£10.00	$15.44	
Jockey			£10.00	$15.24	
Jockey			£6.01		
Jockey	1990s		£5.01		
Jockey			£4.99	$7.61	
Jockey	1990		£5.00	$7.72	
Jogger			£9.61	$14.84	
Jogger			£17.00		
Jogger	1980s		£15.59	$23.76	Square Feet
Jogger				$53.27	Square foot
Jogger			£200		Pointed foot
Jogger			£4.99	$7.61	
Jogger	1980s		£16.03	$24.75	
Judge	1998		£4.30		
Judge			£2.99	$4.56	
Juggler			£2.20	$3.40	
Juggler			£8.00	$12.35	
Juggler			£4.00	$6.18	
Juggler			£5.00	$7.72	
Juggler			£6.50	$10.04	
Juggler			£00.00	$9.99	
Juggler			£2.20	$3.35	
Juggler			£3.70		
Juggler			£4.00		Mint
Juggler	Early			$9.99	
Juggler	Early			$9.99	
Juggler				$5.50	Large
Juggler	1990s		£3.75		
Juggler			£4.00	$6.10	
Juggler			£4.99		
Juggler			£4.99		
Juggler			£4.99		
Juggler			£4.99		
Juggler			£4.99	$7.61	
Juggler			£4.99	$7.61	
Juggler			£4.00	$6.18	
Juggling				$9.99	
Karate			£3.50		
Karate			£6.10	$9.30	
Karate	1993/4		£4.70	$7.16	
Karate				$5.00	Large

Name	Date	Series	GB£	US$	Description
Keep Fit			£4.00	$6.18	
Keep Fit			£4.99	$7.70	Vg Condition
Keep Fit	1990s		£2.39		
Keep Fit			£5.00	$7.72	
Keep Fit			£5.37	$8.29	Mint in bag
Keep Fit			£6.50	$10.04	Mint
Keep Fit	1990		£4.00	$6.18	
Keep Fit			£4.20	$6.48	Small, mint in bag
Keep Fit	1990		£4.99		
Keep Fit	1990		£4.99		
Keep Fit			£3.70		
Keep Fit			£4.00	$6.10	
Keep Fit			£4.99		In VG condition
Keep Fit			£4.99	$7.61	In VG condition
Keep Fit			£8.00		Large
Keep Fit				$5.00	Large
Knight	1996		£3.50		
Knight	1996		£5.20		
Knight	1996			$7.70	
Knight				$14.50	
Knight			£3.20	$4.88	
Lemon				$24.99	
Lemon				$15.00	
Lemon				$15.00	
Lemon	Vintage			$23.50	Mint
Lemon	Pre-war		£114.00		2 Lemons with Golly face
Lemon			£102.00		Bubble
Lemon			£570		Silver Shred in a scroll, only 150 made, White Scroll
Lemon			£570		Silver Shred in a scroll, only 150 made, Blue Scroll
Lifeboatmen			£42.02		
Lifeboatment			£60.00		
Lledo Model T Ford			£4.99	$7.70	
Lledo DG13 Ford A Van				$6.00	MIB
Lledo DG3 Hd Van				$6.00	Marmalade MIB
Lledo DG43 Morris Van				$7.50	MIB
Lollipop Man			£30.00		
Lollipop Man			£40.00		Big Eyes
Lollipop Man	1980			$86.00	
McGolly	1990s		£45.00	$68.59	With rarer White Sporan and Tassle
McGolly			£8.00		
McGolly	1990		£7.00		
McGolly	1990		£16.00	$24.39	
McGolly				$9.99	
McGolly			£4.99		
McGolly			£4.99	$7.61	
McGolly			£4.99	$7.70	
McGolly			£4.99		
McGolly			£3.50		
McGolly			£4.20		
Milkman			£16.00		
Milkman			£21.00		
Milkman	1980			$20.00	
Milkman	1980s			$15.99	
Milkman	1980s		£20.00		
Milkman	1980			$29.99	
Millennium	2000		£11.01		Mint
Millennium	2000			$202.00	
Millennium	2000		£166		Silver, Limited Edition of 2000
Miller			£9.02	$13.75	Silver Shred

Name	Date	Series	GB£	US$	Description
Miller	1950			$42.00	
Miller			£9.02	$13.93	Silver Shred
Mincemeat Poster			£5.00	$7.72	
Motor Bike Racing	1980		£5.19		
Motor Cyclist			£10.52	$16.24	
Motor Cyclist			£8.50		
Motorbike			£4.99		
Motorbike			£5.19		
Motorbike			£12.50	$19.05	
Motorbike			£4.99		
Motorbike			£7.60	$11.58	
Motorcycle	1980			$8.00	
Motorcycle				$40.00	Rare Colour
Motorcyclist	1980s		£12.50	$19.30	
Motorcyclist			£5.53		
Motorcyclist			£7.50		
Mountie			£11.00	$16.98	
Mountie + Advert	1996		£26.00		
Mountie			£4.99		
Mountie			£4.53		
Mountie			£6.19		
Mountie	1980			$8.00	
Nurse			£16.00	$24.70	
Nurse	1990		£5.51	$8.51	
Nurse			£3.50	$5.34	
Nurse			£4.90	$7.47	
Nurse	1980s		£10.56		Red Cross
Nurse	1980s		£4.50		With Red Cross
Nurse	1980s		£6.50		Red Cross
Nurse	1980s		£7.01		
Nurse	1980s		£3.00		MIB
Nurse	1980s		£5.85	$8.92	MIB
Nurse				$10.00	Large V Green
Nurse			£8.00		
Nurse	1990s		£5.50		
Nurse			£4.80		
Nurse			£4.99		
Nurse			£7.00	$10.67	
Nurse			£7.50	$11.43	
Olympic (x 4) Set	1992	Barcelona	£120		
Olympic Games Set	2000		£76.00		
Orange	1980		£56.06		
Orange	Pre-War			$152.50	Golly face among orange and green leaves
Organic Farmer			£5.51		
Organic Farmer			£9.50	$14.48	
Original			£4.00		
Original			£4.00		
Painter				$9.99	
Painter				$9.99	
Painter				$9.99	Mint
Paper Boy	1996			$41.02	
Paper Boy	1996		£10.00	$15.44	
Paper Boy	1996		£4.21		
Paper Boy	1996		£5.75		
Paper Boy			£7.90	$12.04	
Pilot			£10.50	$16.21	
Pilot			£5.00	$7.72	
Pilot			£4.00		
Pilot			£8.51		
Pirate	1996		£40.56		

Name	Date	Series	GB£	US$	Description
Pirate	1996		£35.00		
Plane	1900s		£4.99	$7.61	
Pocket Golly Calender	1960		£4.20	$6.48	
Policeman			£6.51	$10.05	
Policeman	1990		£5.00	$7.72	
Policeman			£4.99		
Policeman			£6.51	$9.92	
Policeman			£8.00		Large
Policeman			£4.42		
Policeman				$6.00	Large
Policeman	1990s		£4.20		
Policeman			£4.00		
Policeman			£4.00		
Policeman			£4.99		
Policeman			£4.99	$7.61	
Policeman			£4.99	$7.61	
Policeman			£8.00		
Policeman	1990		£5.00	$7.72	
Policeman			£6.00		
Policeman	1990		£70.55		Blue shirt
Postman (GPO)			£11.00	$16.77	
Postman (GPO)			£4.99		
Postman (GPO)			£4.99		
Postman	1980		£11.01		Nice
Postman	1980s		£16.00	$24.39	
Postman			£13.00		
Postman	1980			$19.00	
Postman			£8.50		
Queen				$9.99	
Queen				$9.99	
Queen				$9.99	Mint
Queen	1999		£7.50		MIB
Ra Ra Girl			£4.32	$6.58	
Race Car Driver			£8.50		
Racing Car Driver			£10.50	$16.01	
Racing Car Driver			£4.00		
Racing Car Driver			£4.99		
Racing Car Driver				$7.51	Large H
Racing Car Driver Cloth			£6.69		
Racing Driver			£6.65	$10.14	
Racing Driver Cloth Patch	1970s		£14.50	$22.39	
Raspberry				$24.99	
Raspberry				$24.99	
Raspberry	Vintage			$15.50	
Raspberry			£25.00		Fattorini
Rev	1950			$59.19	Gomm
Rev	1970			$45.00	Gomm, Rare
Rev	1970			$42.00	Gomm
Roman			£5.19	$7.91	
Roman			£5.19	$8.01	Mint
Roman	1999		£7.02		MIB
Rudolf & Santa			£25.01		
Rugby Player			£11.51	$17.54	
Rugby Player				$5.70	Large Thin
Rugby Player			£4.20		
Rugby				$7.55	Large H
Runner			£6.55	$10.11	
Runner			£6.55	$9.98	
Safari			£3.00	$4.63	1920s on it, in Suit

Name	Date	Series	GB£	US$	Description
Sailor	1980s		£20.00	$30.88	Mint in bag
Sailor			£24.26	$36.98	
Sailor			£4.99		
Sailor			£20.01		
Sailor	1980s		£26.00	$40.14	
Santa and Reindeer			£30.00	$45.73	With box
Santa				$59.00	Staff issue
Saxophone Player Figure	1998		£4.20		
Saxophone Player Figure			£5.50	$8.49	
Saxophonist			£2.99	$4.56	
Scarecrow			£3.70	$5.64	
Scarecrow	1996		£4.21		
Scarecrow	1996		£4.32		
Scarecrow	1996			$6.50	
Scarecrow				Au $20.00	
Scout			£10.00	$15.44	
Scout				$10.49	Rare
Scout			£10.00	$15.24	
Scout			£5.00		
Scout			£8.66	$13.20	
Scout	Old			$24.99	
Scout				$16.50	Gomm
Scout			£7.50	$11.43	
Silver Crane Bike Toast Rack			£50.00	$77.20	
Silver Crane Golf Cup/Mug			£100.00	$154.40	
Silver Crane Skateboard Cup			£86.00	$132.78	
Silver Crane Teapot			£226.00	$348.94	
Silver Farewell			£28.35	$43.21	Mint
Silver Farewell				$44.99	
Silver Golly			£166.00	$253.03	Limited Edition Silver Millennium
Silver Shred Fridge Magnet			£2.50	$3.86	
Singer			£4.21	$6.42	
Singer	1998		£5.50		
Skateboard	1990		£4.00	$6.18	
Skateboard	1990s		£7.50		
Skateboard			£4.99	$7.61	
Skateboard			£4.99	$7.61	
Skateboard	1990		£7.00		
Skateboarder			£3.21		
Skateboarder			£8.00		Mint
Skater				$10.95	
Skater			£4.19	$6.47	
Skater			£12.70	$19.36	F&S
Skater			£5.00		Fattorini
Skater	1970s		£33.02		Y.W.
Skier			£5.20	$8.03	
Skier			£4.00	$6.18	
Skier				$5.50	Large
Skier	1990s		£3.20		
Skier			£37.05		Bubble
Skier			£4.00		
Skier			£4.99	$7.61	
Skier			£4.99	$7.61	
Skier			£7.50		Mint
Skier	1980			$61.00	Bubble
Skier			£6.75	$10.42	
Skiing				$9.99	
Snooker Player			£22.07		
Snooker Player	1980s			$19.99	
Snooker Player	1980			$42.00	

Name	Date	Series	GB£	US$	Description
Snooker Player	1980s		£23.00	$35.51	
Space Hopper				$9.99	Mint
Spaceman				$9.99	
Spaceman			£4.99		
Spaceman			£5.00		
Spaceman			£4.05		
Standard	1970		£9.51		
Standard	1980s		£2.20		
Standard			£10.50	$16.01	F&S
Standard			£32.11	$48.95	J R Gaunt
Standard			£5.50	$8.38	
Standard	1990s		£5.50		
Standard			£10.01		
Standard			£10.50	$16.01	
Standard			£3.50	$5.34	
Standard			£3.50	$5.34	
Standard			£4.99	$7.61	
Standard			£4.99	$7.61	Classic pose
Standard			£7.77	$11.84	
Standard			£10.00	$15.24	Golden Shred
Standard	2000		£4.99	$7.61	
Standard				$5.00	Large
Standard			£3.00	$4.63	1930 on it
Standard			£5.50	$8.49	
Standard			£5.50	$8.49	
Standard			£5.51		
Standard	1980			$10.00	
Standard	1950			$38.00	Fattorini & Sons
Standard			£4.00	$6.18	
Standard	1980s		£7.50	$11.58	
Standard	1950s		£4.00	$6.18	
Standard Cloth Badge			£5.19		
Standard Figure			£8.50	$13.12	
Stewardess				$5.00	Large
Strawberry		Fruit	£41.83		
Strawberry			£72.51		Bubble
Surfer			£5.61	$8.55	
Surfer	1990s		£4.71		
Surfer			£10.50	$16.21	
Surfer			£5.50	$8.49	
Surfer				$5.50	Large
Surfer			£3.41	$5.20	
Swimmer			£4.80	$7.32	
Swimmer				$5.00	Large
Swimmer	1993/6		£9.50		(H)
Swimmer			£4.99		
Swimmer			£4.99	$7.61	
Tennis Player				$15.50	
Tennis Player			£8.54	$13.02	
Tennis Player			£7.50		Girl
Tennis Player	1990s		£3.27		
Tennis Player			£14.50		
Tennis Player			£17.52		
Tennis Player			£5.00		
Tennis Player	Old -		£23.78		Rare
Tennis Player			£22.99		
Tennis Player			£8.01		W/W
Tennis Player			£4.99	$7.61	
Tennis Player			£6.50	$9.91	
Tennis Player			£6.70	$10.34	
Tennis Player	1970s		£5.51	$8.51	Cloth Patch

Name	Date	Series	GB£	US$	Description
Tennis			£4.99		
Tennis			£5.19		
Tennis	1970		£14.99		Gomm
Thank Golly Its Friday Mug			£9.50	$14.67	
T.G.I.F Mug			£14.51	$22.40	
Thin Chef			£8.27	$12.61	
Torch Bearer		Barcelona	£16.05	$24.47	
Torch Bearer	1992	Barcelona	£16.00	$24.70	
Train Driver			£31.00		Vintage Golly Badge
Train Driver			£12.53		
Trick or Treat		Golidays	£7.00		
Trumpet Player Figure			£5.50	$8.49	
U.S. Soccer	1980			$8.00	
Union Jack			£10.00	$15.24	Repro
Viking	1996		£4.40		
Viking	1996		£5.50		
Viking	1996			$8.26	
Viking			£10.00		
Viking			£3.20	$4.88	
Viking			£10.50		
Viking			£7.51	$11.60	
Waiter	1998		£5.21		
Waiter			£4.01	$6.11	
Waiter			£4.99		
Waving			£4.99		
Waving			£4.99		
Weightlifter			£4.95	$7.55	
White Tin Button			£1.40	$2.13	
White Tin Button			£1.20		
White Tin Button			£2.72		
White Tin Button			£3.70		
White Tin Button			£7.00		
White Tin			£2.21		
White Waistcoat				$24.99	White waistcoat
Wizard			£8.50	$13.12	
World Cup 2002			£11.00	$16.77	England Golly Badge with flag
World Cup 2002			£16.00	$24.39	England Golly Badge
World Cup 2002			£17.00	$25.91	
World Cup 2002			£18.01	$27.45	England Golly Badge
World Cup 2002			£30.00	$45.73	England Golly Badge
World Cup 2002			£31.50	$48.02	England Golly Badge
World Cup 2002			£33.00	$50.30	England Golly Badge
World Cup '98			£60.01		
World Cup '98			£80.00		In box
Wren				$9.99	
Wren	1996		£3.92		
Wren	1996			$9.26	
Wren			£5.51	$8.40	
Wren			£3.70		
Yellow Tin Button			£1.40	$2.13	
Yellow Tin Button			£3.70		
Yellow Tin Button			£6.30		
Yellow Tin Button			£1.40		
Yellow Tin Button			£2.66		
Yellow Tin			£2.00		

Robertson's Golly Jeans Patches

Set of 15 circular jeans patches issued in 1977.

Accordian Player
Balloonist
Drummer
Fisherman
Footballer
Guitarist
Horserider
Lollipopman
Motorcyclist
Racing Driver
Standard
Sax Player
Skateboarder
Tennis Player
Yachtsman

Balloon Championship circular jeans patch issued 1977.
One arm raised Golly patch cut to shape of Golly 1985
Price £15+ each.

1920s Perfumery and Compact items. Glass scent bottle modelled as a Golly. French origin. Glass scent stopper and bakelite Golly rouge compact.

1960s Robertson's Golly Chair £200-£225/$295-$345.

Childs golly chair, 21inches high with a tubular frame made in Surbiton, Surrey and issued as a Robertsons golly offer in 1969.

Two of the many plastic golly shopping bags issued by Robertsons. Yellow Shopping Bag, £15-£25/$20-$40; Red Shopping Bag, £10-£20/$15-$30.

Miscellaneous Gollies

A Robertson's hot water bottle dating from the 1980s. £10-£20/$15-$30.

Robertson's Golly Radio, £25-£30/$35-$45.

Jeans patches £15/$22 each.

Miscellaneous Gollies

Set of five Musician thimbles. £40-£50/$60-$75.

A selection of keyrings including the Ballet dancer and Jet pilot from 1993, The Baseball player from 1990, A circular "Golly it's Good" and a standard Golly fridge magnet. Keyrings, £10-£20/$15-$30 each.

Miscellaneous Gollies

Hand knitted Golly Jumper knitted using a Robertson's pattern from 1981. £10/$15.

Vigny "Gollywog" perfume made in Paris between 1920s and 1950s. All are very collectable being collected by both golly and perfume collectors. This is a later example of a bottle of eau de cologne. £200-£225/$295-$345.

Golly candy tin made in Australia around the 1950s together with two rather rare golly shaped teething rings from the early 1900s. One made of silver and the other made of brass, both with bone rings. Silver Teething rings, £175/$260+; Golly Tin, £80/$120.

Miscellaneous Gollies

A selection of golly candy tins and tin moneyboxes produced in the1950-70s by Huntley & Palmer. Money/letter box tin £45-£60/$65-$90; Green triangle Golly tin, £80/$120; Selection of Golly Toffee tins £30/$45+; Salt and Peppers £250-£275/$370-$20.

Selection of Robertson's premiums from the 1980s including jigsaw puzzle, pencils, pencil tops and a wooden pencil box given away free with two jars of preserves in Australia. Robert's Jigsaw, £20/$30+; Pencilheads, £3-£5/$5-$7; Pencil box £5/$7+; assorted pencils £3-£4/$5-$6; Plastic head and shoulders Eggcup from boxed set of two £30-£35/$45-55.

Tiny 1960s golly alarm clock which was also made in white, along with a 1980s golly wall clock. Both were issued by Robertson's. £225-£250/$335-$385.

Robertsons issue wall clock, made of wood and available in the 1980s.

In 1977 Robertsons sponsored a balloon festival at Castle Howard, Yorkshire. Due to bad weather the balloons could not leave the ground never the less the festival was a great success. A festival program was issued featuring the golly balloons and golly balloon brooches were also sold.

Record £125/$185+.

Robertsons Golly Eggcups; Sailing Club £45/$65; Golly in Doorway, £20-£25/$30-$55; plastic head and shoulders Golly from boxed set of tw
£30-£35/$45-$55; Drummer £45/$65.

Miscellaneous Robertsons Golly items.

Pelhams Golly Puppets.

Golly jigsaws by Victory Puzzles.

Fake Carlton Ware

Worthless fakes. These gollies are imitations of the original Carlton/Robertsons gollies previously illustrated. The Carltonware logo on the reverse is also fake. As counterfeits, theare like fake money – WORTHLESS. If you see anyone selling these as originals – they are breaking the law, and commiting a criminal offence.

A collectors note

Eve Rossiter, major contributor to the Golly Collectors Handbook

Born and educated in Cambridgeshire, England, Eve is married with one child, a dog and a cockatoo. She has always had a fascination with golly, from her first golly doll as a child through to the 1950s, and she collects Robertsons brooches to the present day. Her interest in golly was renewed in the 1970s with the birth of her son, Andrew and for the past 30 years she has been an enthusiastic researcher into the history of golly with a special interest in Robertsons. She has an extensive collection of golly memorabilia and loves to share her knowledge. For this reason she has created her own website, GollyWorld. Eve would be pleased to hear from fellow collectors who would enjoy sharing their knowledge and she can be contacted via her website
at: www.GollyWorld.co.uk

She says:
"My mother used to save tokens from Robertson's preserves so that I could send off for their famous golly badges. In later life I created a website on the internet, dedicated to golly and named it GollyWorld so I could share my collection and make lots of golly friends with a similar passion.

The golly character is a happy image and I have to thank James Robertson for bringing him into my home. Although golly retired from Robertsons last year, he is still going strong with collectors, around the world, golly clubs have been set up, badges made and beautiful dolls created by talented artists.

I hope this book will bring as much pleasure to readers as it has been for me to have been part of the team that created it.